# The Mouse in the Forest

### by Susan Buonafiglia
### illustrated by Janet Skiles

 HOUGHTON MIFFLIN    BOSTON

There is a big old log deep in the forest. Something lives in the log, deep in the forest.

A mouse has a nest in the old log.  It made its nest with lots of twigs, grass, and soft, green moss.

The mouse leaves its nest in the
evening. Where do you think it's going?
What will it do?

The mouse is looking for things to eat.
It likes to eat nuts, seeds, leaves, and the
buds on plants.

Now the mouse sits up. It is cleaning its face. The mouse's tail helps it sit up.

Then the mouse runs along a little trail through the forest. Who do you think made the trail?

Many of the mice who live in the forest
made the trail with their small feet. They
used their feet to pat down grass and plants.

9

Other small animals run on the trail
too.  See the hungry fox creeping on the
trail near the mouse.  Can the mouse hear
the hungry fox?  What will the mouse do?

The mouse runs fast on its strong legs.
It jumps and climbs too. It gets away from
the hungry fox.

The mouse runs back to its nest. It is safe there. It will rest all day.

Sleep well, little mouse!